B1 Writing

Ten practice tests for the **Cambridge B1 Preliminary**

Anna Phillips and Terry Phillips

PROSPERITY EDUCATION

© Prosperity Education Ltd. 2025

Registered offices: Sherlock Close, Cambridge
CB3 0HP, United Kingdom

First published 2025

ISBN: 978-1-915654-49-6

Original edition © Innova Content Ltd.

This publication is in copyright. Subject to statutory exception
and to the provisions of relevant collective licensing agreements,
no reproduction of any part may take place without the written
permission of Prosperity Education.

This edition is published by arrangement with Innova Content Ltd.

The moral rights of the authors have been asserted.

'Cambridge B1 Preliminary' and 'PET' are brands belonging to The
Chancellor, Masters and Scholars of the University of Cambridge and are not
associated with Prosperity Education or its products.

Designed by ORP Cambridge

For further information and resources, visit:
www.prosperityeducation.net

To infinity and beyond.

Contents

Introduction   *v*

Test 1   *1*

Test 2   *7*

Test 3   *13*

Test 4   *19*

Test 5   *25*

Test 6   *31*

Test 7   *37*

Test 8   *43*

Test 9   *49*

Test 10   *55*

Answers   *61*

Bonus content: B2 Reading practice test x 2   *73*

A digital platform for Cambridge exam preparation

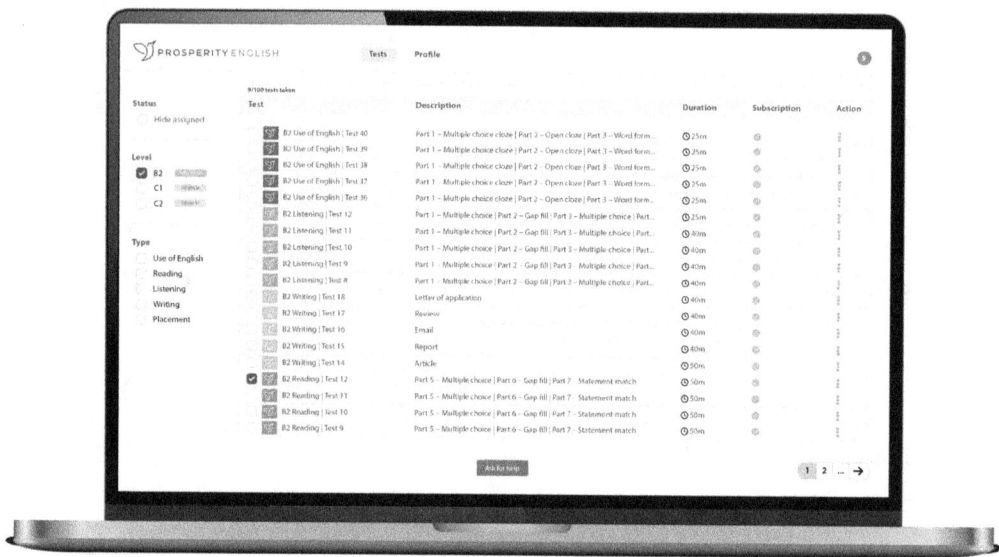

Prosperity English provides ample opportunities for repetitive practice, allowing you to reinforce your learning and improve your exam skills steadily.

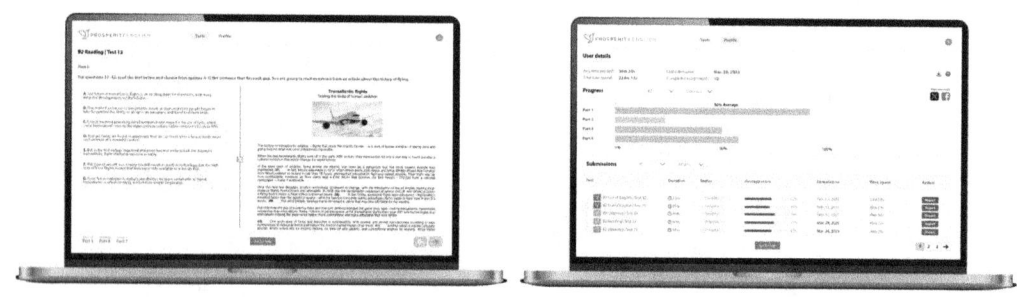

Try it for free

www.prosperityenglish.com

40% promotional discount code:
TIAB40

Introduction

Welcome to this edition of sample tests for the Cambridge B1 Preliminary Writing, which has been written to replicate the Cambridge exam experience and has undergone rigorous expert and peer review.

The B1 Preliminary English language exam is the third of six levels established in the Common European Framework of Reference (CEFR): A1–C2. Candidates of all ages can take the B1 Preliminary test. In the exam you will have 45 minutes to complete the Writing paper. This section has two parts, and is worth 25% of the final score.

You can take the B1 Preliminary exam on a computer or on paper. The content is the same for both forms of the test. The B1 Preliminary Writing paper gives you the opportunity to show your language skills. The topics of tasks are chosen so that they are relevant to the typical student taking this exam, so you should find that you have enough ideas to write about. Each question will guide you by identifying the context, the purpose for writing and the target reader.

It is important to remember that you aren't being tested on the subject content of the tasks. So, if the topic of the Part 1 question, for example, is education, you aren't expected to be an expert about this topic. The test format is:

	Number of questions	Number of marks	Task types	What do candidates have to do?
Part 1	1	20	An email	Write about 100 words, answering the email and notes provided. Candidates are assessed using four subscales: Content, Communicative Achievement, Organisation and Language.
Part 2	1	20	Choice between an article or a story	Write about 100 words, answering the question of their choosing. Candidates are assessed using four subscales: Content, Communicative Achievement, Organisation and Language.
Total	2	40		

For more information, visit the Cambridge Assessment English website.

Read the Part 1 question carefully, and make sure that you understand what each of the four notes refers to. Read both of the Part 2 questions. There will be two questions, and you will need to choose one. When making your choice, you will need to think about the task type, the topic and the language that you will need.
It is good advice to spend time thinking about each question before you start writing. If you start one question and then realise that you don't feel confident about the ideas or language you need, you may need to change question.

This book contains 10 Reading tests (Parts 1–6), comprising a total of 320 individual assessments. You or your students, if you are a teacher, will hopefully enjoy the wide range of texts and benefit from the repetitive practice, something that is key to preparing for this part of the B1 Preliminary (PET) examination.

We hope that you will find this resource a useful study aid, and wish you all the best in preparing for the exam.

Cambridge B1 Preliminary

Writing

Test 1

© 2025 Prosperity Education.
'Cambridge B1 Preliminary' and 'PET' are brands belonging to The Chancellor, Masters and Scholars of the University of Cambridge and are not associated with Prosperity Education or its products.

Part 1

You **must** answer this question.
Write your answer in about **100 words**.

Question 1

Read this email from a friend, Jo, and the notes you have made.

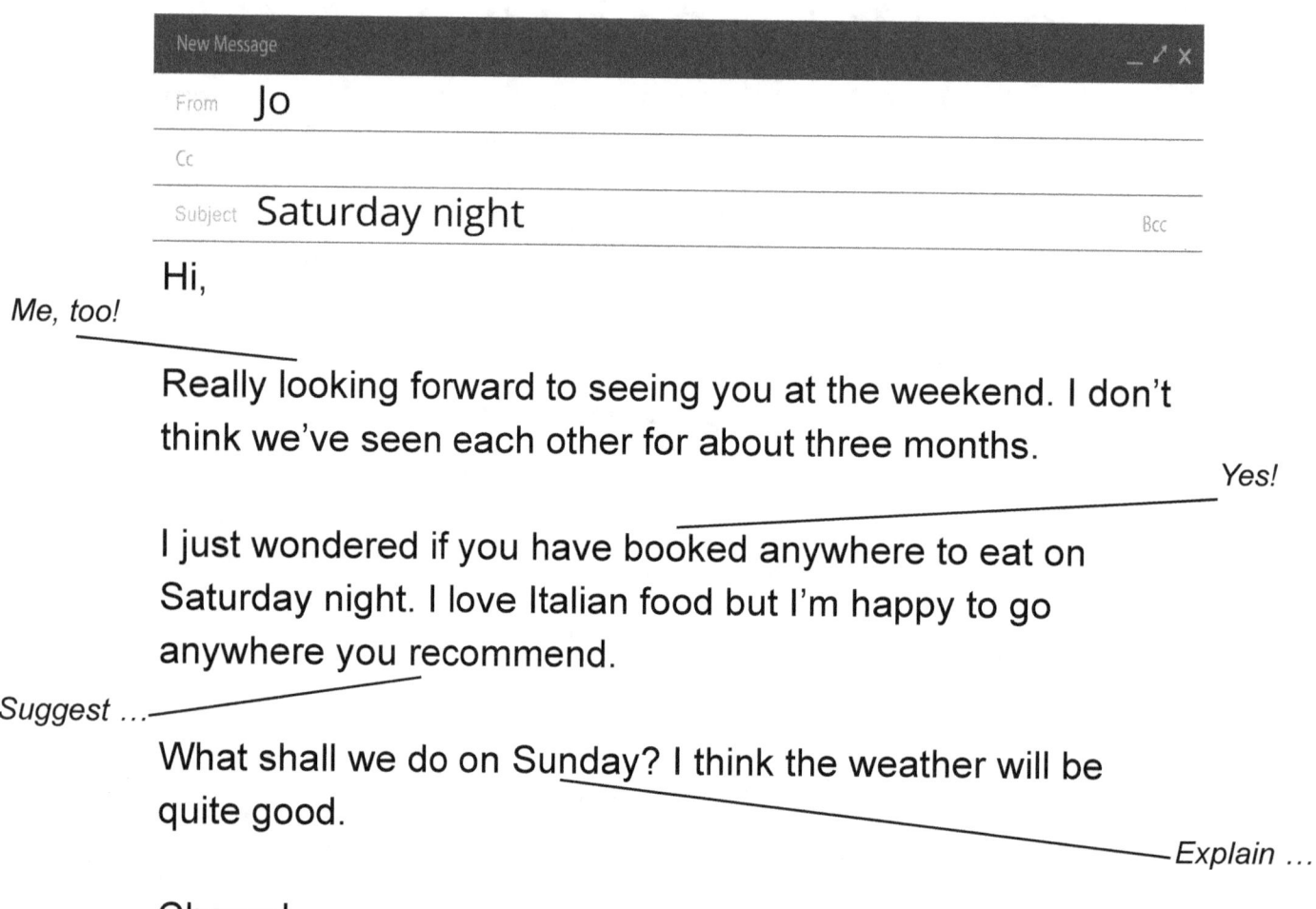

Write your **email** to Jo using **all the notes**.

Part 1

Part 2

Choose **one** of these questions.
Write your answer in about **100 words**.

Question 2

You see this announcement in your school English-language magazine.

Articles wanted!

WHAT IS YOUR FAVOURITE KIND OF FICTION?

Why do you like those books?

What kind of novels don't you like? Why?

Write an article answering these questions and we will publish your work.

Write your **article**.

Question 3

Your English teacher has asked you to write a story.

Your story must begin with this sentence.

Leah arrived at the house and found the front door open.

Write your **story**.

Part 2 Question 2

....

....

....

....

....

....

....

....

Part 2 Question 3

....

....

....

....

....

....

....

Cambridge B1 Preliminary

Writing

Test 2

© 2025 Prosperity Education.
'Cambridge B1 Preliminary' and 'PET' are brands belonging to The Chancellor, Masters and Scholars of the University of Cambridge and are not associated with Prosperity Education or its products.

Part 1

You **must** answer this question.
Write your answer in about **100 words**.

Question 1

Read this email from your teacher, Mr Collins, and the notes you have made.

New Message

From: **Mr Collins**
Cc:
Subject: **Geography quiz**

Dear Students,

— Good idea!

This is to let you know that we will have a world quiz during the geography lesson next Tuesday.

— Write …

Could you please email me three questions about your own country which you think your classmates might be able to answer? For example, the population or the location of the country.

Give answers

Make sure you give the answers to your questions in case I don't know them!

I'm not sure whether we should do the quiz in teams or not. Which would you prefer?

Reply

Michael Collins

Write your **email** to Mr Collins using **all the notes**.

Part 1

Part 2

Choose **one** of these questions.
Write your answer in about **100 words**.

Question 2

You see this announcement in your school English-language magazine.

Articles wanted!
MY BEST FRIEND Who is your best friend? Why? Where did you meet your best friend? **Write an article answering these questions and we will publish it next month.**

Write your **article**.

Question 3

Your English teacher has asked you to write a story.

Your story must begin with this sentence.

We were crossing the desert when the car suddenly stopped.

Write your **story**.

Part 2 Question 2

Part 2 Question 3

Cambridge B1 Preliminary

Writing

Test 3

© 2025 Prosperity Education.
'Cambridge B1 Preliminary' and 'PET' are brands belonging to The Chancellor, Masters and Scholars of the University of Cambridge and are not associated with Prosperity Education or its products.

Part 1

You **must** answer this question.
Write your answer in about **100 words**.

Question 1

Read this email from your friend, Alice, and the notes you have made.

New Message

From: Alice
Cc:
Subject: Sue's birthday party
Bcc

Hi,

How are things?

It's getting close to Sue's birthday, so I thought we'd better catch up! I've bought the present which we all agreed on. I'm sure she'll love the perfume! — *Thanks!*

Have you managed to book the restaurant yet? If not, you'd better do it soon, because it's sometimes difficult to get a table for seven on a Saturday. — *There are 8 of us!*

Also, what about the cake? I think you said you were happy to make it, but I know that you've been ill. I'll buy one instead if you haven't got time. — *Yes, please!*

Have we forgotten anything? Let me know!

Need card — you or me

Best,
Alice

Write your **email** to Alice using **all the notes**.

Part 1

Part 2

Choose **one** of these questions.
Write your answer in about **100 words**.

Question 2

You see this announcement in your school English-language magazine.

Articles wanted!

THE MOST INTERESTING PERSON I HAVE MET

Who is the most interesting person you have ever met?

Where did you meet, and why do you find him or her so interesting

Write an article answering these questions and we will publish it next month.

Write your **article**.

Question 3

Your English teacher has asked you to write a story.

Your story must begin with this sentence.

It was getting dark and there was a huge tree across their path.

Write your **story**.

Part 2 Question 2

Part 2 Question 3

Cambridge B1 Preliminary

Writing

Test 4

Part 1

You **must** answer this question.
Write your answer in about **100 words**.

Question 1

Read this email from your English friend, Ben, and the notes you have made.

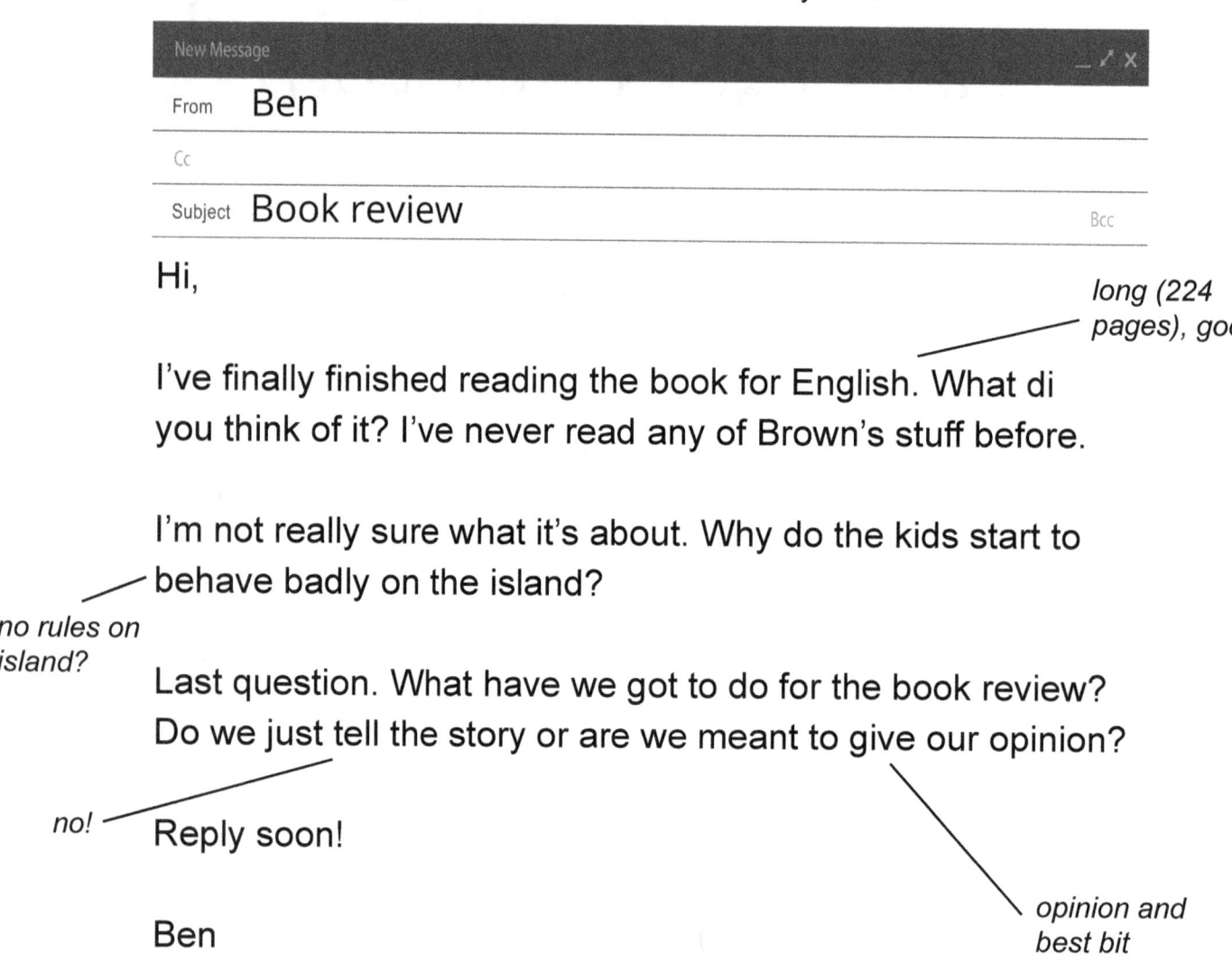

Write your **email** to Ben using **all the notes**.

Part 1

Part 2

Choose **one** of these questions.
Write your answer in about **100 words**.

Question 2

You see this announcement in your school English-language magazine.

Articles wanted!
MY HOBBY What is your favourite hobby? When did you start it and why do you enjoy doing it? **Write an article answering the questions and we will put it on our website.**

Write your **article**.

Question 3

Your English teacher has asked you to write a story.

Your story must begin with this sentence.

He heard the terrible noise again.

Write your **story**.

Part 2 Question 2

Part 2 Question 3

Cambridge B1 Preliminary

Writing

Test 5

Part 1

You **must** answer this question.
Write your answer in about **100 words**.

Question 1

Read this email from your drama teacher, Ms Marsh, and the notes you have made.

From	Head of Drama
Cc	
Subject	School play

Dear Students, — *Great!*

The school play this year will be *Oliver Twist* by Charles Dickens – a musical version written specially for us by Miss Green, your English teacher!

If you would like to take part in the play, please reply to this email and say whether you are interested in a large or small part. — *Large!*

If you would like to be considered for a large part, please give details of the previous parts you have played. — *main part last year in Treasure Island*

Please note that ALL the large parts have songs, so you must be able to sing well. — *singer in rock group*

I need your emails by the end of this week.

Ms Marsh

Write your **email** to Ms Marsh using **all the notes**.

Part 1

Part 2

Choose **one** of these questions.
Write your answer in about **100 words**.

Question 2

You see this announcement in your school English-language magazine.

Articles wanted!
MY BEST TEACHER Who has been the best teacher in your education so far? What subject(s) does he or she teach? Why do you think this teacher is the best? **Write an article answering these questions and we will put it on our website.**

Write your **article**.

Question 3

Your English teacher has asked you to write a story.

Your story must begin with this sentence.

The wind was getting stronger and pushing the tiny boat out to sea.

Write your **story**.

Part 2 Question 2

Part 2 Question 3

Cambridge B1 Preliminary

Writing

Test 6

© 2025 Prosperity Education.
'Cambridge B1 Preliminary' and 'PET' are brands belonging to The Chancellor, Masters and Scholars of the University of Cambridge and are not associated with Prosperity Education or its products.

Part 1

You **must** answer this question.
Write your answer in about **100 words**.

Question 1

Read this email from your science teacher, Mr Martin, and the notes you have made.

New Message

From: **Mr Martin**
Cc:
Subject: **Science project**

Dear Students,

As you know, we have an annual Science Fair at the school. This year it will be on June 14th

[Note: Great! Enjoyed last year]

Students from Year 10 will work in groups of three. I need to know who you will be working with, and their class numbers.

[Note: Vicky Scott (10C), Harry Smith (12C) and me]

I also need a good name for your team.

[Note: Waterworks]

At the fair, you must present an experiment which demonstrates a principle of chemistry or physics. Just let me know the principle you will be demonstrating, NOT the actual experiment. We can discuss that in the next science class.

[Note: Water pressure increases with depth]

Please let me have your reply before the end of the week!

Tom Martin
Head of Science

Write your **email** to Mr Martin using **all the notes**.

Part 1

Part 2

Choose **one** of these questions.
Write your answer in about **100 words**.

Question 2

You see this announcement on your school English-language film website

---

Articles wanted!

WHAT IS YOUR FAVOURITE FILM?

What is it about and why do you like it?

What's your favourite part? Why?

Write an article answering these questions and we will publish your work.

Write your **article**.

Question 3

Your English teacher has asked you to write a story.

Your story must begin with this sentence.

My father shouted, 'Get inside – we've got about a minute until it gets here!'

Write your **story**.

Part 2 Question 2

Part 2 Question 3

Cambridge B1 Preliminary

Writing

Test 7

© 2025 Prosperity Education.
'Cambridge B1 Preliminary' and 'PET' are brands belonging to The Chancellor, Masters and Scholars of the University of Cambridge and are not associated with Prosperity Education or its products.

Part 1

You **must** answer this question.
Write your answer in about **100 words**.

Question 1

Read this email from a friend, Poppy, and the notes you have made.

New Message

From: **Poppy**
Cc:
Subject: **End of year party**

Hi,

Sam told me that you are in charge of the party. Sorry, I didn't know. I was ill last week. —— *better now?*

I'm happy to help if you still need anything. I could make sandwiches or organise the drinks. —— *Yes!*

Suggest ... —— Or I could do anything else you want, although I'm not very good at cooking!

If you want me to buy anything, please let me know how much I can spend. I suppose there is some money left in the party funds which we all contributed to? —— *Explain ...*

Poppy

Write your **email** to Poppy using **all the notes**.

Part 1

Part 2

Choose **one** of these questions.
Write your answer in about **100 words**.

Question 2

You see this announcement on your school English-language film website.

> **Articles wanted!**
>
> ### THE BEST DAY OF MY LIFE
>
> What has been the best day of your life?
>
> When did it happen? Why was it so good?
>
> **Write an article answering these questions and we will publish your work.**

Write your **article**.

Question 3

Your English teacher has asked you to write a story.

Your story must begin with this sentence.

The alarm hadn't gone off and now Suzi was late.

Write your **story**.

Part 2 Question 2

Part 2 Question 3

Cambridge B1 Preliminary

Writing

Test 8

Part 1

You **must** answer this question.
Write your answer in about **100 words**.

Question 1

Read this email from your geography teacher, Mr Haynes, and the notes you have made.

From: Mike Haynes
Cc:
Subject: Local area studies

Dear Students,

I'm writing to ask you for information about the next geography project, which is due in shortly. — *When?*

You need to work in groups of three, and I must know the names and classes of your group as soon as possible to ensure that everyone in Year 10 is working in a group.

Mae Green (10A), Ben Simms (10C) and me!

As you know, the topic is local area studies. Your group must choose a building or an area which has changed significantly over the last 50 to 100 years. Please let me know what you have chosen and why, when you are ready.

How many words?

If you need any more information before you begin work, ask me now!

Mike Haynes
Head of Geography

Weston House – was luxury hotel, now flats

Write your **email** to Mr Haynes using **all the notes**.

Part 1

Part 2

Choose **one** of these questions.
Write your answer in about **100 words**.

Question 2

You see this announcement on your school English-language film website.

> **Articles wanted!**
>
> ## WHAT IS YOUR FAVOURITE SUBJECT?
>
> What subject is your favourite and why do you like it so much?
>
> Are you planning to continue to study the subject in the future? Why?
>
> **Write an article answering these questions and we will publish your work.**

Write your **article**.

Question 3

Your English teacher has asked you to write a story.

Your story must begin with this sentence.

It was the day of Oliver's 12th birthday, but he wasn't feeling very excited.

Write your **story**.

Part 2 Question 2

Part 2 Question 3

Cambridge B1 Preliminary

Writing

Test 9

© 2025 Prosperity Education.
'Cambridge B1 Preliminary' and 'PET' are brands belonging to The Chancellor, Masters and Scholars of the University of Cambridge and are not associated with Prosperity Education or its products.

Part 1

You **must** answer this question.
Write your answer in about **100 words**.

Question 1

Read this email from a classmate, Sofia, and the notes you have made.

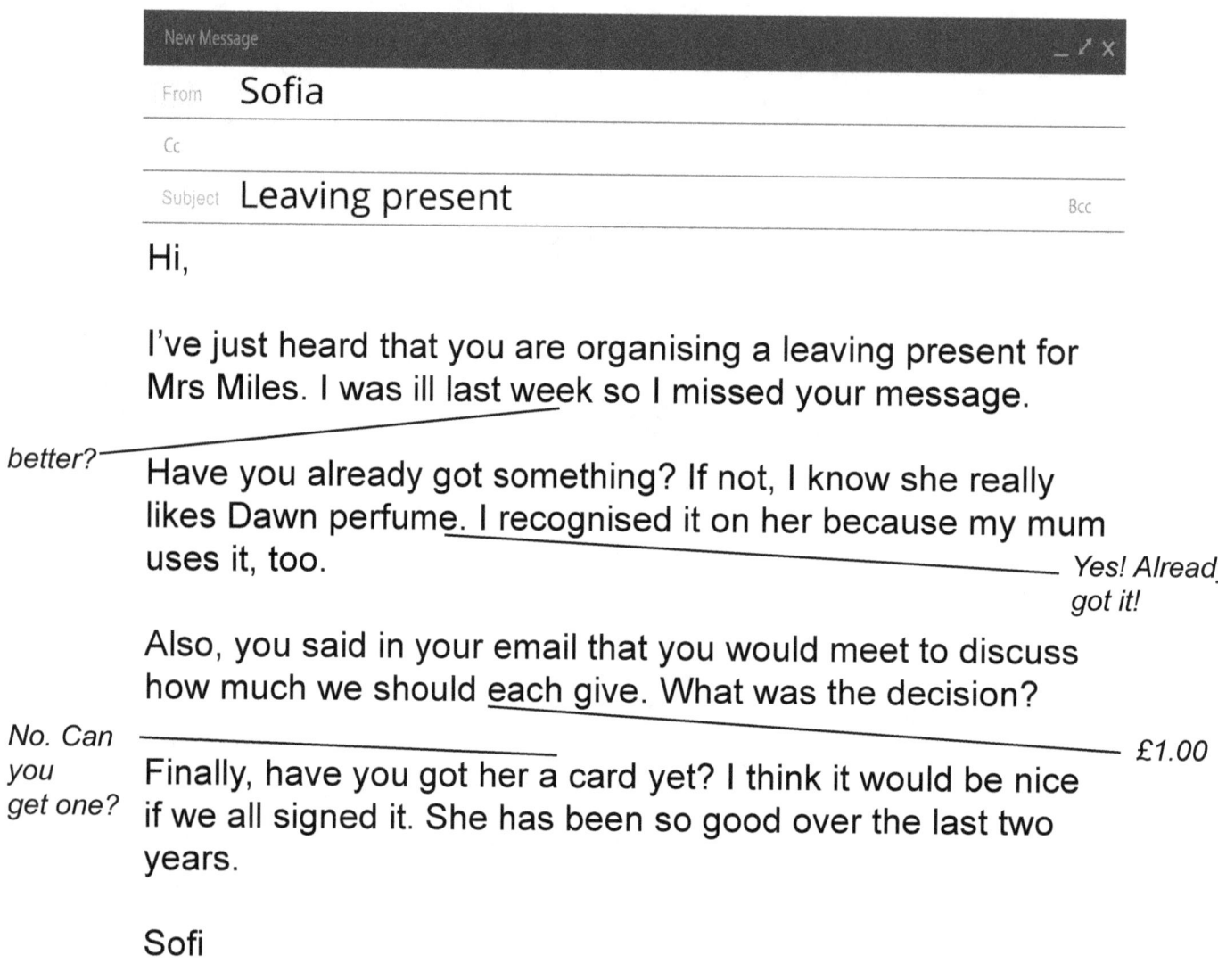

Write your **email** to Sofia using **all the notes**.

Part 1

Part 2

Choose **one** of these questions.
Write your answer in about **100 words**.

Question 2

You see this announcement on your school English-language film website.

Articles wanted!
WHAT IS YOUR BEDROOM LIKE?   Where in the house is your bedroom?   Why do you like it? What don't you like about it?   **Write an article answering these questions and we will post your work.**

Write your **article**.

Question 3

Your English teacher has asked you to write a story.

Your story must begin with this sentence.

George was feeling really sad as he put the last few things in his suitcase.

Write your **story**.

Part 2 Question 2

Part 2 Question 3